THE YOUNG JOURNALIST'S BOOK

HOW TO WRITE AND PRODUCE YOUR OWN NEWSPAPER

Donna Guthrie and Nancy Bentley

Illustrated by Katy Keck Arnsteen

The Millbrook Press • Brookfield, Connecticut

Published by The Millbrook Press, Inc.
2 Old New Milford Road, Brookfield, Connecticut 06804

Copyright © 1998 Donna Guthrie and Nancy Bentley
Illustrations © 1998 Katy Keck Arnsteen
All rights reserved
Printed in the United States of America
1 3 5 4 2

Library of Congress Cataloging-in-Publication Data
Bentley, Nancy.
The young journalist's book: how to write and produce
your own newspaper/Nancy Bentley and Donna Guthrie;
illustrated by Katy Keck Arnsteen.
p.   cm.
Includes index.
Summary: Describes the various functions and elements of a newspaper,
giving practical advice on writing, producing, and distribution.
ISBN 0-7613-0360-X (lib. bdg.)
1. Journalism—Authorship—Juvenile literature.   2. Newspaper publishing—Juvenile
literature. [1. Newspapers.]   I. Guthrie, Donna.   II. Arnsteen, Katy Keck, ill. III. Title.
PN4776.B46 1998   070.1'72—dc21   97-43692   CIP   AC

TABLE OF CONTENTS

INTRODUCTION

What Is News?

North, South, East, West. News comes from all directions. News is information about real people, places, and events.

As far back as ancient Egypt, where slaves gathered news for the Pharaoh, people have been curious about what is happening.

In medieval Europe, town criers walked through the streets shouting out important events of the day. Later, messengers rode on horseback from town to town delivering news about recent battles or the coronation of a new ruler.

About 1450, Johann Gutenberg invented movable type that made printing on paper cheaper and faster. The invention of the printing press led to the widespread creation of newspapers, called gazetteers.

These large, one-page broad sheets looked like posters. They informed citizens about the comings and goings of ships, the names of the ships' captains, and what each ship carried.

Today, news is gathered, written, and delivered via radio, television, computers, electronic media, and the daily newspaper. People who write the news are called journalists. Each day a crew of editors, reporters, photographers, and printers work to bring the news of the world to you.

Are you curious about the people and the world around you? You can become a journalist, too. This book is a step-by-step guide on how to gather information, analyze facts, write stories, and create a newspaper for your family, class, or school.

HOW ARE NEWSPAPERS DIFFERENT FROM BOOKS?

A book is written to be read again and again.

A newspaper is written to be read once.

Books can be about imaginary people, places, and things.

Newspaper stories are about real people, places, and events.

Books are written in the first, second, or third person point of view.

Newspapers are usually written in the third person point of view.

Books can be about issues from the past, present, or future.

Newspapers must be about issues that are new or timely.

Books can be any length and are filled with details and long sentences.

Newspaper stories are filled with short, simple sentences.

WHAT IS A JOURNALIST?

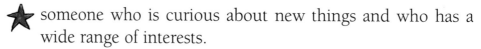

A journalist is:

★ someone who is curious about new things and who has a wide range of interests.

★ someone who can view various sides of a situation and present the facts fairly.

★ someone who understands other people, and knows what they care about.

★ someone who can take complicated ideas and facts and write about them clearly.

★ someone who can sift through many facts and present only the important ones.

★ someone who wants to explain a new fact, a new issue, or a new idea to other people.

Always carry a pencil and pad. Be ready to jot down the facts of your next news story.

Observant eyes see a story in the making.

A nose for news can smell a story a mile away.

A speedy hand can write detailed notes while the story is breaking.

A questioning mouth has "who, what, when, where, why, and how" on the tip of its tongue.

Open ears listen for the real story and hear the facts.

A NEWSPAPER STAFF

 The *publisher* organizes the editorial, printing, and distribution of the newspaper.

 The *editor* decides which stories are newsworthy and assigns each story to a reporter. When the story is written the editor evaluates and edits the reporter's work.

 The *reporter* gathers the facts and writes the story.

 The *photographer* takes the pictures that will add interest to the story. A reporter who also takes pictures is called a *photojournalist*.

 The *cartoonist* draws either cartoons or comic strips.

 The *copyreader* or *proofreader* checks all spelling, grammar, and punctuation.

 The *designer* uses the computer to lay out each page of the newspaper, including headlines, columns, photographs, and advertisements.

 The *printer* makes copies of the newspaper and distributes them to readers.

Selling ads in your newspaper can help pay for the costs of printing and mailing.

SEVEN STEPS TO CREATING A NEWSPAPER

Here are the steps involved in creating a newspaper:

STEP SEVEN

STEP SIX

STEP FIVE

STEP FOUR

STEP THREE

STEP TWO

STEP ONE

1. Decide what's newsworthy.
2. Gather the facts and research both sides of the story.
3. Write the story.
4. Proofread the story.
5. Lay out the page by adding clip art and photographs.
6. Print the newspaper.
7. Distribute the newspaper.

WHAT IS NEWSWORTHY?

In 1882, Charles A. Dana of the *New York Sun* said: "When a dog bites a man, that is not news; but when a man bites a dog, that *is* news."

As a reporter, it is impossible to write about everything. Besides, your readers won't be interested that your mother grows pumpkins in her garden, that your teacher read a book to your class, or that your friend likes to tap-dance. That's not news.

But if one of your mother's pumpkins weighs 700 pounds (318 kilograms) and takes the blue ribbon at the state fair, *that's* news!

If your teacher wrote the book that she is reading to you, and the characters came from people in your class, *that's* news!

And if your friend joins 6,000 other tap dancers in New York City to dance down 34th Street to break a world record, *that's* news!

As a reporter you must learn to recognize what makes a good news story.

Look for stories that are:
Timely   True
Unusual   Interesting

GATHER THE FACTS AND RESEARCH THE STORY

When you are asked to cover a news story, do research by collecting facts on the scene.

A good news reporter will:

⭐ observe the event.

⭐ ask questions.

⭐ be accurate about time and place.

⭐ record people's reactions and opinions.

⭐ spell names correctly.

You can also use the library for research. Read books, encyclopedias, magazines, and newspapers to verify your facts.

At the library, you can also listen to taped interviews and watch video documentaries. Examine computer databases, photographs, and maps. Ask permission to log on to the Internet and search the web for information.

When you are asked to do a feature story you will have more time to do in-depth research. There are two types of sources for research: primary and secondary.

1. A primary source is a person speaking or writing about his or her own life. Primary sources include:

- ⭐ personal experiences
- ⭐ interviews
- ⭐ original diaries and journals
- ⭐ newsreels
- ⭐ documentary videos

2. A secondary source takes primary information and puts it in another form.

For instance, Eleanor Roosevelt's diaries are primary sources, but a biography about Eleanor Roosevelt is a secondary source.

THREE TYPES OF NEWSPAPER STORIES

Newspaper stories are of three basic types:

news stories

feature stories or human-interest stories

editorials

News stories about recent events are also called "hard news" and can be found on the front page of every newspaper. They are timely—written one day and published the next.

Feature stories and human-interest stories are also called "soft news" and can be found inside the newspaper. These stories are meant to entertain and inform. They are usually about the people and places behind the hard news.

The editorial column is the publisher's soapbox.

Editorial stories voice opinions about recent events in the news. They appear on the editorial page. This is where the editor or reporter uses hard facts to present his or her personal point of view. These short essays raise tough questions, try to set the record straight, or persuade the reader to think or act in a certain way.

WRITING A NEWS STORY

Newspapers are read by busy people who want to know the facts as quickly as possible. That's why a news story is different from other stories you will write.

 A news story is always factual.

 The first paragraph of your news story usually answers the questions: Who, What, Where, When, Why, and How in the order of importance for that story.

 News stories are brief, concise, and easy to read.

 News stories are often written one day and published the next.

Remember – all news stories should be written in the third person. Do not use I, My, We, Us, Me, or Our.

JOURNALISTIC STYLE

A good news story is more than a collection of facts. Newspaper writing requires a sense of style. Style hooks your reader's interest by using simple words to tell the facts accurately and in order. Choose words that are easily understood and familiar to the reader. Avoid clichés!

Keep each paragraph under six lines. In order to write this way, remove all unneeded words.

Last Saturday morning, just before the big rainstorm, the very big, bad-mannered Belvedere Wolf strolled down to Swine Crest Court, to the large oak tree, which grows in front of the shaky stick home of Mr. Amos Pig. Mr. Wolf, showing his well-known bad temper, blew, and blew, and blew the house down on the head of the little pig who was hiding under his Super Pig bedspread.

Tighten to read:

On Saturday morning Mr. Belvedere Wolf blew down the stick home of Mr. Amos Pig.

INTERVIEWS

Interviews make a story come alive.

First determine what you need to know. Then decide who can give you that information. Call the person, introduce yourself, and politely make an appointment for an interview.

Before the interview:

★ Make a list of questions.

★ Check to see if your tape recorder works and bring extra batteries.

★ Dress appropriately.

★ Arrive early.

During the interview:

★ Be polite.

★ Observe everything about the person.

★ Take notes.

★ Practice abbreviating or skipping words when taking notes.

★ Ask permission to use your tape recorder.

★ Turn your tape recorder on and put it to the side.

★ Look directly at the person.

★ Ask the person to please repeat if you don't understand what he or she said.

★ Stay on schedule and focused on the subject.

★ Thank the person for his or her time.

Ask open-ended questions that start with Why, What, or How. Avoid questions that can be answered with a simple Yes or No.

Ask questions that involve the senses: "How do you feel?" "What did you see?" "Who did you hear?" After long quotes, ask the person if what you wrote is what he or she meant. Then reread your notes to them.

Ask your most important question halfway through the interview, when the subject is relaxed and comfortable talking to you. Finish the interview by asking, "Is there anything you'd like to add?"

After the interview:

 Listen to your tape.

 Transcribe your notes.

 Jot down your observations.

When the story is published send a copy to the person you interviewed.

QUOTES

What a person says is called a *quote*. It brings a human element to a news story. Quotes can be gathered on the scene when the story happens or during an interview.

Quotes make good leads or can be added to the body of your story.

Quotes must always have a source. It is important to tell the reader who said what. This is called *attribution*. It's important to give attribution or credit to the person whose words you use. Otherwise the reader will assume the newspaper or the reporter is the source.

Use quotation marks when you quote someone word for word. This is called a *direct quote*.

"I've never been as proud of my mother as when I saw her graduate from college this year," said Lily Jane McAfee, age nine.

When you paraphrase or shorten what a person says, do not use quotation marks. This is called an *indirect quote*.

One of the proudest days in her life, according to Lily Jane McAfee, is the day her mother graduated from college.

THE NAME GAME

People like to read about other people. Stories that include names of people are more interesting to read.

A story that says, "An opera singer broke a window while on stage" isn't as interesting as "Ms. Tina Travalari, famous Metropolitan Opera singer, shattered a nearby window when she hit high C."

Stories without names aren't very interesting. Names add human interest. As a journalist, it's your job to get the names and spelling correct and to attribute the story to the correct person. Even "Smith" can be spelled "Smythe"— always ask.

The first time you use a name in a story, use the entire name:

Mr. John Jacob Jingelheimer Schmitt is the president and founder of the new "Whistle While You Work" club.

Throughout the rest of the story, you can use just the last name:

Mr. Schmitt and his group of five whistling woodworkers were removed from City Hall yesterday when they disrupted a meeting.

Good writers try to avoid repetition. Use the person's name only once in a paragraph.

PYRAMID

In most fiction stories, you tell your reader a few facts at a time and build to a conclusion. For instance, if you were writing a mystery, you would sprinkle clues throughout your story. By the end of the mystery, your reader could put all the clues together and find out "who did it."

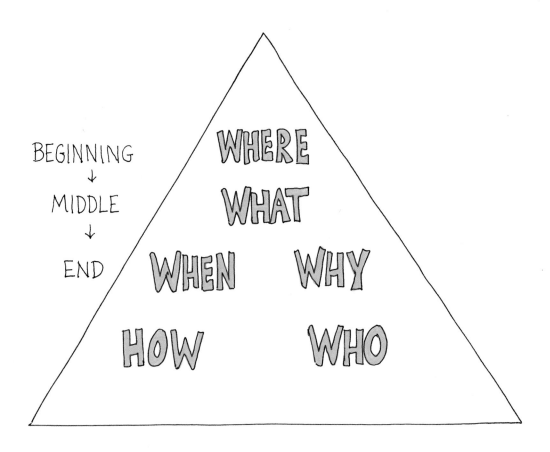

BEGINNING
↓
MIDDLE
↓
END

WHERE
WHAT
WHEN   WHY
HOW   WHO

INVERTED PYRAMID

In a news story, you tell your reader the important facts in the first paragraph. This is called the inverted pyramid style. If the reader wants more details about the story, he or she reads on.

The *inverted pyramid* is used by journalists because:

⭐ reporters know that this is an easy way to tell a story.

⭐ reporters can write stories faster.

⭐ editors can easily create a headline after reading the first paragraph.

⭐ the reader can quickly decide if he or she wants to read on.

When newspaper space is limited, an editor can cut the end of the story and not omit the important facts.

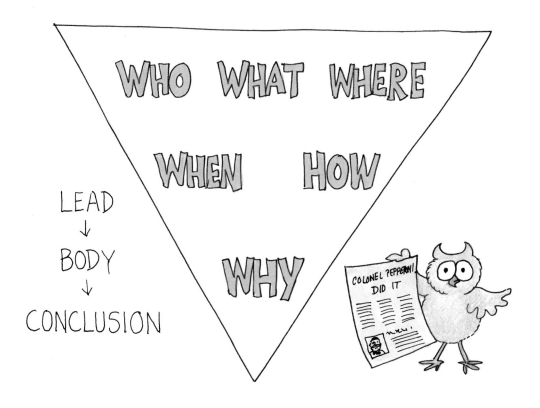

BLUEPRINTS FOR NEWS STORIES

When the great Pharaohs built a pyramid, they used a set of plans, or a blueprint. A journalist uses a blueprint, too.

The elements of a news story are:

LEAD

The first paragraph gives the essential details of the story and "hooks" the reader to read on.

BODY

The middle paragraphs of the story answer the questions Who, What, When, Where, Why, and How. They include quotes and the names of the people in the story.

CONCLUSION

The last paragraph of the story summarizes the story and gives the reader something to think about.

BEGINNING

LEADS

Strong leads are usually less than twenty words.

A lead is the first sentence in the first paragraph of a news story. It is designed to hook the reader's interest. The lead tells the reader quickly what the story is about and helps the editor create the headline. It takes practice to write a good lead.

To write a good lead, ask yourself: "What does this story mean?"

Pick the most interesting fact and put it right at the beginning. Write a simple, precise summary sentence. That is your lead. There are several types of leads. Here are a few examples.

Standard Lead: Good standard leads have strong, active verbs. They attract attention and add strength to the beginning of the story.

Put action words at the beginning of your lead sentence.

Question Lead: A question will grab the reader's attention and convince him or her to read on.

Quote Lead: A powerful quote gets the reader into the news story by introducing one of the main characters. If it's a direct quote, you must tell who made the statement.

Descriptive Lead: A descriptive lead gives the picture of the situation and draws the reader into the news story.

MIDDLE

THE BODY

The body of a news story elaborates on the facts and fills in background information about the people, places, or events from your first paragraph.

Tell the story in a logical way. Read over your notes to check how and when things happened. It helps to outline your story to decide how many paragraphs you will need.

Each paragraph should begin with a different word, have a strong topic sentence, and a single focus. Sentences should vary in length and structure. Don't clutter your story with too many facts. Use an anecdote, statistic, or quote to support an important point.

The writing should be clear, accurate, and easy to understand. Do not give your opinion, just state the facts. Use names when you quote sources and follow the rules of good grammar.

Remember, there is no good news or bad news, only the facts.

END

CONCLUSION

When you've given full background information about the facts and details reported in the first paragraph, it's time to end the story.

Check the beginning of your story and ask yourself, "Have I answered all the questions a reader might ask? Have I said it well?" It is easy to slip into an opinion or try to draw a conclusion for the reader. Stick to the facts. Go back and polish your grammar and punctuation. End the story with a sentence or two that will make the reader think about what you wrote.

PHOTOGRAPHS

A reporter who takes pictures for the newspaper is called a photojournalist. Instead of a pad and pencil, he or she relies on a camera and film to capture the story. A good photograph will draw the reader's attention to the story.

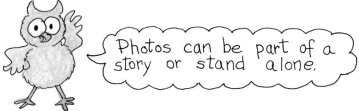

Photos can be part of a story or stand alone.

IDEAS FOR GOOD NEWS STORIES

1. A BABY IS BORN IN THE FAMILY

2. LOCAL POLICE AND BUSINESSMEN HAVE FORMED AN ANTI-GRAFFITI PATROL

3. YOUR SCOUT TROOP IS HAVING A FOOD DRIVE FOR THE HOMELESS

4. THE ROOF OF THE GYMNASIUM COLLAPSED IN A RECENT SNOWSTORM

5. THE TOWN IS WELCOMING DR. WILL SOAR, FIRST MAN TO EXPLORE MARS

6. YOUR GRANDPARENTS ARE CELEBRATING THEIR FIFTIETH ANNIVERSARY

WRITING A FEATURE STORY

You can find feature stories everywhere you find people. Keep your eyes and ears open for the interesting and the unusual. In a news story, the reporter tells just the facts, but the feature writer is a nonfiction storyteller.

For instance, if your school is celebrating its twenty-fifth anniversary, a hard-news story would announce where and when the event is to take place and who is invited. A feature story could be written about the school's first principal, teachers, or graduating class.

Hard-news stories answer the questions Who, What, Where, When, Why, and How. Feature stories focus on one of these questions, usually Who?

A good feature writer will:

 think about the most important person involved in the event.

 interview that person as the focus of the story.

 gather interesting details about the person by talking to family and friends.

 go to the library to find books, magazines, old news stories, and photos about the person.

check computerized databases about the person.

search the Internet for current information about the person.

WRITING A FEATURE STORY

Cluster your ideas into groups or categories. If you're writing a story about a school bus accident, organize the information around the bus or the driver or the passengers, or the place where the accident happened.

 Read through your notes.

 Make a list of subjects.

 Choose one subject for the focus of your story.

 Outline your story.

 Write your story.

IDEAS FOR FEATURE STORIES

1. THE GRANDMOTHER AND GRANDFATHER WHO VOLUNTEERED AT YOUR SCHOOL ARE GETTING MARRIED

2. FRIENDSHIP AROUND THE WORLD VIA THE INTERNET

3. THE ZOO WELCOMES A NEW ELEPHANT AND A NEW ZOOKEEPER

4. A BOY IN YOUR NEIGHBORHOOD INVENTED A FISH TANK CLEANER

5. AN INTERVIEW WITH THE NEWEST TEACHER AT YOUR SCHOOL AND THE TEACHER WHO HAS BEEN THERE THE LONGEST

6. FIVE THINGS YOUR FAMILY CAN DO TO CELEBRATE NEW YEAR'S EVE

WRITING AN OP-ED PAGE

One page in the newspaper is set aside for the personal opinions of the editors, reporters, and readers. It is often called the op-ed page because it includes editorial columns and readers' opinions.

Editorial stories have three parts:

 Lead Paragraph:
Write a strong hook.
Address the situation.
State your opinion.
Present your strongest argument with a set of facts.

 Body:
Present the opposing argument.
Criticize it fairly.

 End:
Repeat your strongest argument.
Draw a conclusion from the facts.
Propose a solution.

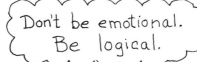
Don't be emotional.
Be logical.

POLITICAL CARTOONS

Political cartoons are drawn by artists to express an opinion about some current event, topic, or problem. You find political cartoons on the editorial pages.

One of the most popular political cartoonists was Thomas Nast. In the 1870s he drew cartoons about corruption in New York City. Today political cartoons are used in newspapers because they make a point quickly and attract a reader's attention.

To draw a political cartoon, you should:

 like to draw.

 have a sense of humor.

 be aware of current events.

 use images rather than words to express yourself.

 use characters to make your point.

express your opinion by exaggerating an aspect of a person or situation.

WRITING AN EDITORIAL LETTER

On the editorial page are letters written by readers. Letters to the editor are reactions and opinions to the stories, articles, or editorials that have been in the paper. Writing a letter to the editor gives the reader a chance to compliment or criticize a certain writer, protest a situation, or clarify the facts.

Your letter to the editor should:

 state the issue.

 describe the situation as you see it.

 show that you are informed by stating the facts.

 propose a solution for improvement or change.

When you write a letter to the editor, always be polite.

IDEAS FOR AN OP-ED PAGE

 1. A political cartoon about the state of school lunches

 2. A letter to the editor about putting a stop sign at the end of your block

 3. An editorial praising students who cleaned up the play-ground on Saturday

 4. An editorial about things every kid can do for the environment

 5. A letter to the editor about the choice of comics in the newspaper

 6. A political cartoon for or against a dress code at your school

SPECIAL SECTIONS

The newspaper is filled with more than just news.

Newspapers are filled with special sections such as sports, travel, movies, reviews, and comics. The stories in these sections are considered soft news and are usually written like feature stories.

The special sections covered in this book are:

 Comics
 Sports Stories
 Travel Stories
 Reviews
 Columns
 Notices and Announcements
 Classifieds

To be a good journalist, study your local newspaper. Which sections do you like best?

Start a notebook with your favorite sports articles, movie reviews, travel articles, and some of your favorite columns. Try to write just like those writers on new topics. By imitating the writing style of good journalists, your newspaper writing will improve. Through practice you will find your own style and voice.

COMICS

Most cartoons are line drawings.

Since the 1890s, cartoonists have been drawing comic strips for newspapers. Comic strips are a form of storytelling. Every story needs characters, a setting, a conflict, and a solution.

In a four-frame comic strip, the first frame sets the scene, while the second and the third frames show action. The last frame delivers the punchline or ending.

Some comic strips are funny, and some are serious. Some show a humorous slice of life each day, while others tell a story that continues for weeks at a time.

FUNNY

SERIOUS

GAG PANEL

POLITICAL CARTOON

A gag panel tells a story with one picture and a caption.

A political cartoon appears on the editorial page because it expresses the cartoonist's point of view. It is usually a single picture that pokes fun or comments on a news event or a current topic.

SPORTS STORIES

Sports stories, like news stories, put the most important information in the first paragraph. The lead is a dramatic sentence to hook the reader. The first paragraph will tell who played and who won.

News reporters can only report the facts, whereas sports writers can use exciting and colorful language such as, "a diamond-edged throw," or "a golden victory."

In the body of your sports story add details about the conditions of the field, the weather, the mood of the crowd, and specifics about key players. Elaborate on the important moments of the game.

Make sure your sports story includes:

⭐ the name of the game.

⭐ where it took place.

⭐ when it took place.

⭐ who (teams or individuals) played.

⭐ the final score of the game.

⭐ highlights of the game.

⭐ information about upcoming games.

Avoid clichés in your sports language, such as "He ran like the wind", or "She jumped for joy when she crossed the finish line."

TRAVEL STORIES

Travel writers love to travel. They are curious about the world and the people in it. When you write a travel article, use your five senses.

In the lead create a vivid picture. In the body of the article tell your readers what sights they will see, what languages they will hear, what foods they will taste, and describe the flowers they will smell.

Start by writing about your hometown. Clip articles from your local paper, visit your local chamber of commerce, and go exploring. If you were a visitor, what museum would you want to see? Where would you go for lunch? Where would you go for a hike? Be honest. Inform your readers about the positive and negative aspects of your town.

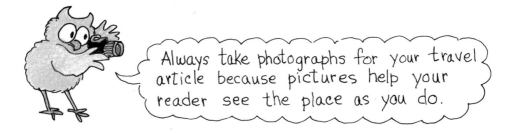

Always take photographs for your travel article because pictures help your reader see the place as you do.

A travel writer needs several tools:

- ⭐ notebook
- ⭐ tape recorder
- ⭐ laptop computer
- ⭐ maps
- ⭐ camera
- ⭐ good walking shoes

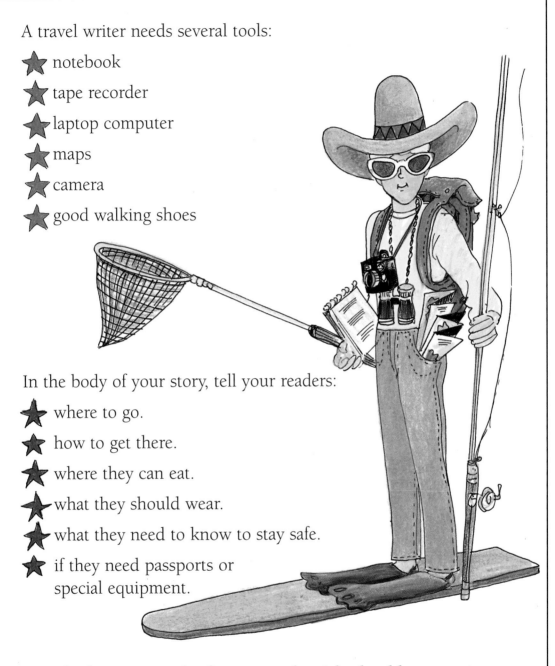

In the body of your story, tell your readers:

- ⭐ where to go.
- ⭐ how to get there.
- ⭐ where they can eat.
- ⭐ what they should wear.
- ⭐ what they need to know to stay safe.
- ⭐ if they need passports or special equipment.

The last paragraph of your travel article should summarize your feelings about the place you visited. Try to inspire your readers to go there and see it for themselves.

REVIEWS
BOOKS, MOVIES, THEATER, AND FOOD

Another name for a reviewer is a critic.

A review is a combination of a news story and an editorial. Give the reader basic information about the book, movie, or play and then write your opinion of it. As a reviewer you have the chance to evaluate television shows, movies, books, the school play, and your Aunt Ethel's pies.

In the lead paragraph of your review, tell the reader what you are reviewing, and when and where you saw it.

Answer these questions:

 Did the author, producer, or playwright tell a good story?

 Was it entertaining?

 Was it worth your time and money?

Reviews are found in the entertainment section of the newspaper.

In the body of your review:

⭐ Summarize the story.

⭐ Give the theme of the movie, book, or play.

⭐ Compare this performance or book with others like it.

⭐ Give your opinion about the performers or characters.

⭐ Support your opinion with specific facts.

At the end of your review, restate your overall opinion and try to persuade your reader to share your point of view.

When you go to a restaurant to review it:

⭐ Go with friends and try lots of things on the menu.

⭐ Evaluate the restaurant's service, atmosphere, and cleanliness.

When you write a restaurant review, include:

⭐ the name, address, and telephone number of the restaurant.

⭐ what you ate and whether or not you liked it.

⭐ the cost of the meal.

COLUMNS

Do you have an interest or a hobby that you would like to write about? Then perhaps you may want to write a column. A column is a short piece about a single subject, written by the same writer, placed in the same spot in the newspaper. It can be written like a news story, a feature story, or an editorial.

Each column should focus on a single topic. For instance, if you're writing a cooking column, all of your columns will be about food. But one day you could write about pizza and the next day about cream pies.

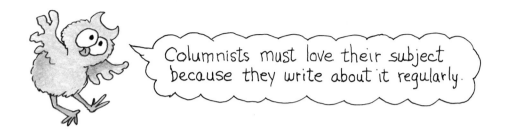

Columnists must love their subject because they write about it regularly.

If you want to be a columnist, think about what interests you. If you love computers and like to share information, consider writing a technology column.

This column might include tips about:

★ new computer equipment

★ computer programs

★ computer magazines

★ computer shows

★ computer books

★ computer games

★ the Internet

★ Web-site designs

Because columns are short, remember to:

★ choose a single idea.

★ list all the points you want to cover.

★ outline the article.

★ create a headline.

NOTICES AND ANNOUNCEMENTS

Birth announcements, engagements, wedding announcements, and obituaries are short, specially formatted messages. Readers provide the information and mail it to the newspaper. The reporter arranges it to fit the newspaper's format and space.

When writing a birth announcement, include this information:

- name and sex of baby
- mother's name and father's name
- place of birth
- date and time of birth
- weight and length of baby, if available
- baby's brothers and sisters

A son, Jordan John, was born to Carrie and John Brown at 5:40 A.M. on May 3, 1998, in Detroit, Michigan. The baby weighed 7 lbs. and 2 oz., and was 19 inches long. He has two brothers, Jonah and Jason, and a sister, Judy.

A wedding announcement should include this information:

 names of the bride and groom

 names of both bride's and groom's parents

 place and date of the wedding

 name of the official who performed the ceremony

 names of those in the wedding party

 reception

honeymoon destination

> Vera Cochran, daughter of Blanche and Stephen Cochran, was married on May 14, 1998, to Luis Garcia, son of Maria and Miguel Garcia at Our Lady of Victory Church. A reception was held at Hero Hall, and the couple took a honeymoon trip to Chicago.

 Each newspaper may have its own style for these announcements.

An obituary should include this information:

 Services were held for *name*, who died at the age of *age*.

 The deceased was born on *date* in the town of *place* and is the son or daughter of (*parents' names*).

 The deceased was known for (*list of accomplishments*).

 He or she is survived by (*names of his or her immediate family*).

> Ismael Long, 85, died October 5, 1998, in Akron, Ohio. He was a bus driver. He is survived by his wife, Sara, and two sons, William and Isaac.

CLASSIFIEDS

At the very end of the newspaper there is a special section called the classified ads. People use the classifieds to find jobs, services, homes to buy, things for sale, lost-and-found items, pets to adopt or buy, and to post personal messages.

Classifieds, also known as want ads, are always in the same place in your newspaper. They are arranged by categories, such as cars, boats, and trucks, or homes for sale, apartments and rooms to rent.

FOR RENT:
2 Bdrm, 1 bath
Apt. 10 South
Street. call
496-3030

FOR SALE:
Boy's bike, 3 yrs
old, and 1 blue
bicycle helmet.
P.O. BOX 2250

LARGE TOM CAT
FOR SALE - $3.00
ALONG WITH
USED CANARY
CAGE : $15.00

Classified ads should be short and to the point. You can use abbreviations for certain words, such as F for female or M for male.

At the end of a classified ad, a telephone number or post office box number is usually used instead of a person's name.

IDEAS FOR THE SPECIAL SECTIONS

1. A column about bike repair

2. A restaurant review of your favorite pizza shop

3. A classified ad to sell your aquarium

4. An interview with the wheel chair athlete of the year

5. A birth announcement for your new kittens

6. A travel article about camping

PROOFREADING AND COPY EDITING

After the reporters have written their stories, they turn them over to a copy editor. This person is expected to correct grammar, spelling, and style, and may also look for errors of fact and cut stories that are too long.

Here are some common copy-editing marks.

ADVERTISING

More readers = more money!

Advertising is one way that newspapers make money. Businesses pay newspapers to advertise their products. The cost of an ad is based on the number of readers and subscribers the paper has. You can cover the cost of your newspaper by selling ads to local businesses. Charge by the size of the ad. The bigger the ad, the more expensive it will be. Classified ads are usually purchased by individuals. The number of lines in a classified ad determines its cost.

Set a limit on how much advertising you will accept. A good rule is that no more than 30 percent of your newspaper should be set aside for ads.

NEWSPAPER LAYOUT

A newspaper page contains several visual elements, all of which are arranged to make the page attractive and easy to read. These elements are the masthead, headlines, bylines, stories, photographs, and captions.

★ Masthead: A masthead is the name of the newspaper. It contains the newspaper's logo, and the date, edition, and price of the paper. These words are often used in newspaper mastheads: Press, Ledger, Times, Gazette, Banner, Herald, News, and Telegraph.

★ Banner Headline: A banner is the main headline on the front page of the paper.

★ Headline: A headline is a short sentence at the top of a story. It grabs the reader's attention by being short, powerful, and giving the main message of the story. Headlines make a page look more attractive. They are written by copy editors and are usually the largest type on the page.

★ Byline: A byline is the name of the person who wrote the story. It goes under the headline.

★ Caption: A caption is a sentence or two that identifies all the people, places, or events in a picture.

HELPFUL HEADLINE HINTS:
Use action verbs.
Avoid words like A, An or The.
Use short words or phrases.
Use a comma in place of and.

The Times

MASTHEAD

LOGO

BANNER HEADLINE

SMITH FOUND GUILTY

JURY TAKES TEN HOURS

PHOTOGRAPH

PRISONER BREAKS DOWN

CAPTION

WINTER
ICE STORM
COMETH

HEADLINE

BYLINE

TRAFFIC GROWS

Mayor Bozzi Bosses Council

The standard newspaper is 14 to 15 inches (36 to 38 centimeters) wide, and 20 to 22 inches (51 to 56 centimeters) high. The standard tabloid newspaper is 10 by 16 inches (25 by 40 centimeters). Your newspaper will probably be printed on letter- or legal-size paper because these papers are less expensive and easy to find.

Here are some tips for laying out your newspaper:

★ Place the most important stories in the upper right-hand section of the paper. That's where people look first.

★ Don't "bump heads" or put two headlines together.

★ Use a photograph on the front page for the lead story.

★ Insert subheadings if the story is long.

★ Use boxes around text to emphasize a story and create variety.

Don't use photos side by side unless there's a relationship between them.

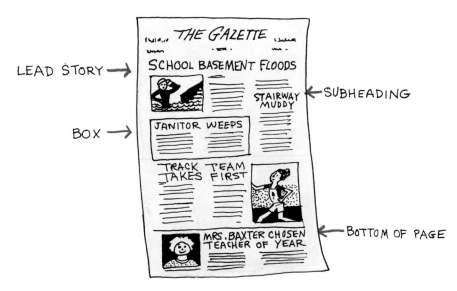

Most newspapers use computers to lay out their pages. By using a computer program you can quickly create the masthead, headlines, bylines, stories, photographs, and captions and easily move them around to lay out your pages.

With a digital camera and color scanner, you can drop photographs or drawings into your pages. Then just enlarge, crop, or move them around. Desktop publishing programs can make your newspaper look professional.

Here are just a few of the programs that are available for creating your newspaper.

Adobe Pagemaker

Student Writing and Research Publishing Center by The Learning Company

You be the Reporter by The Society of Visual Education

The Rookie Reporter by Meridian Creative Group

The Author's Tool Kit by Sunburst Communications

Press Writer by Broderbund

PRINTING

Now you need to make copies of your newspaper. You can print copies using your computer. But if you want to make more than fifty copies, consider taking a clean, clear copy of your newspaper to your local print or copy shop and have copies made there. The more copies you make, the cheaper they will be.

When you choose your paper, consider color and weight. Heavy, textured, or colored paper is more expensive than regular white copy paper.

DISTRIBUTION

Now it's time to put your newspaper in the hands of your readers. This is called distribution. It is the last step in publishing your paper.

Hand-deliver your newspaper to friends and family. It will save you money.

If you are writing a school newspaper, leave copies in the library, computer room, and school office. Distribute your newspaper along with another publication, like the official school newsletter. This way your newspaper will be circulated to more readers.

If you are writing a family newspaper, take copies to family gatherings like your grandfather's birthday party, Thanksgiving dinner, or the annual family reunion.

If you are writing a community newspaper, drop off copies at the community center, local restaurants, libraries, and banks. Before you leave copies of your newspaper in public places, ask the person in charge for permission.

Think about transmitting your newspaper via E-mail, or creating your own Website so that interested readers can download your newspaper.

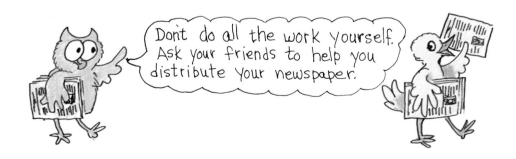

Don't do all the work yourself. Ask your friends to help you distribute your newspaper.

SUBSCRIPTIONS

For people out of town who want to keep reading your newspaper, consider selling a subscription. A subscription is payment in advance for a set number of issues.

Include a subscription form in every newspaper. Put the price of your newspaper above the masthead. Try to keep your subscription fee low. Charge just enough to cover the cost of printing and mailing.

Keep a list of your loyal readers. They may want to subscribe.

Congratulations! Your newspaper is finished.

You've done your best to gather the facts and skillfully weave them together to shape informative and interesting stories.

Ask yourself:

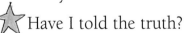

★ Have I told the truth?

★ Have I been accurate?

★ Have I been objective and fair in my story?

★ Have I backed up all controversial ideas and debates with facts and evidence?

★ Have I been considerate of the beliefs and feelings of other people?

Extra, extra!
Read all about it.
Your newspaper's done,
And it's time to shout it!

You've researched each story,
Gathered facts here and there;
You've presented both sides,
Been objective and fair.

You wrote a tight lead,
Were accurate and true;
You answered the questions,
What, When, Where, and Who.

You interviewed newsmakers,
Attributed each quote,
Considered their feelings,
In the stories you wrote.

Now hold up your paper,
And say, "This is mine!
I'm a budding young journalist,
And that's my byline!"

INDEX